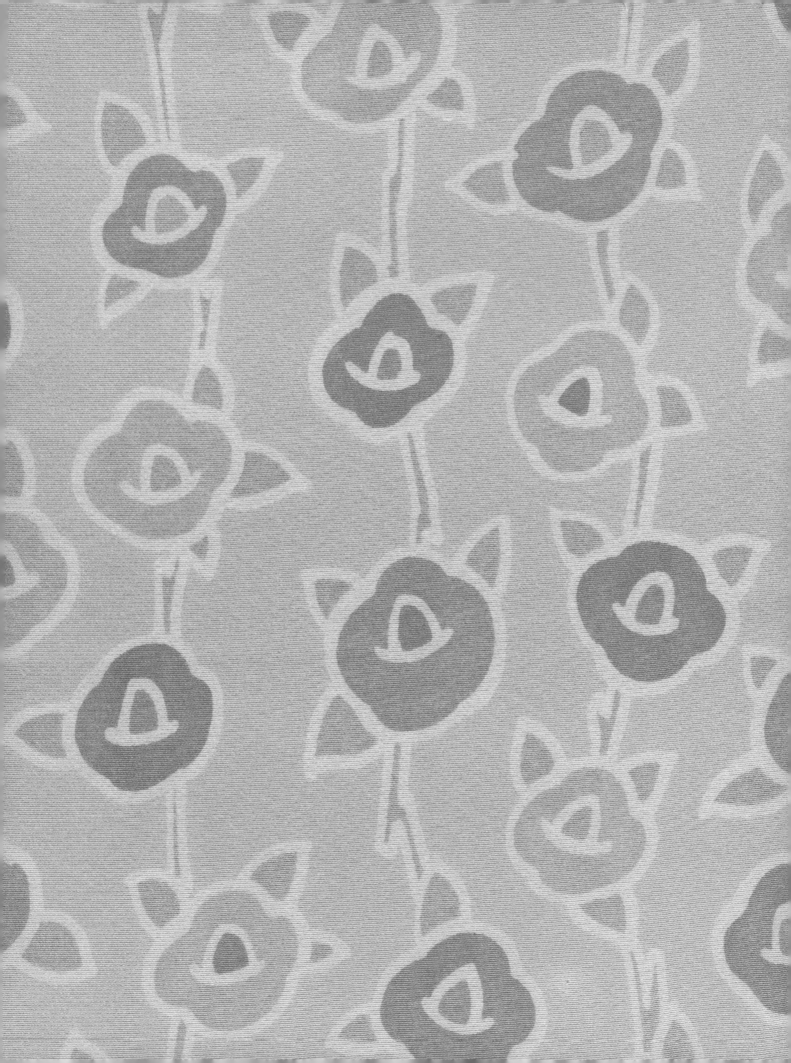

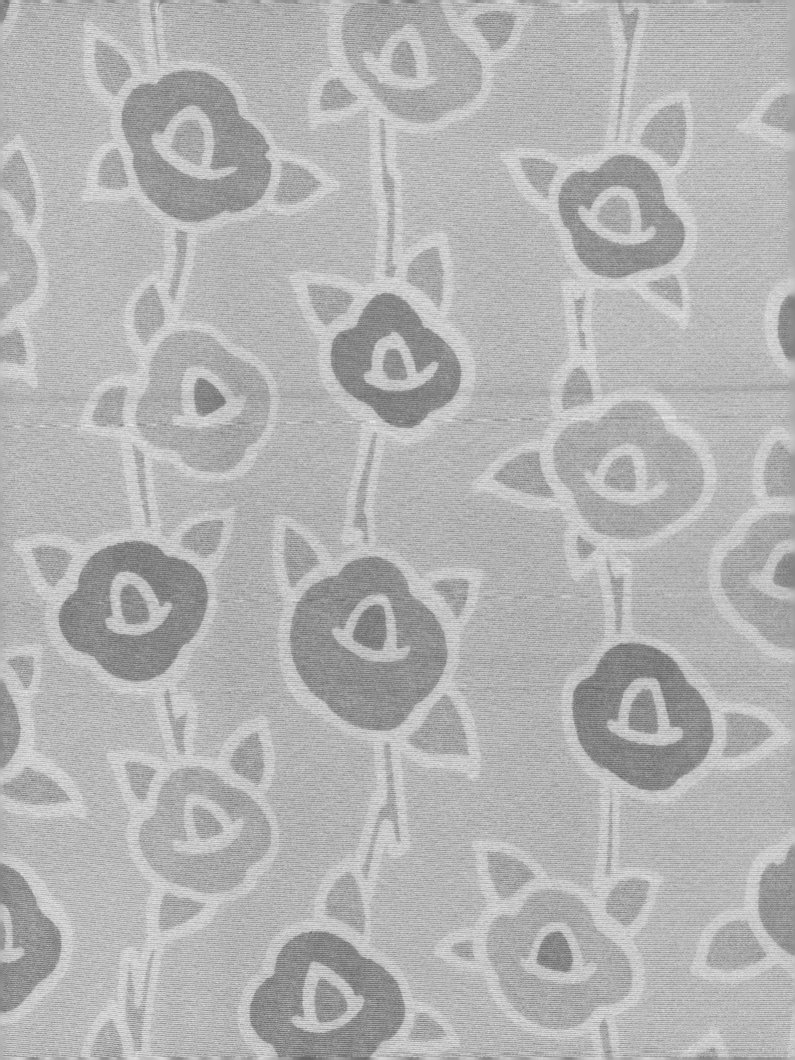

QUILTING
with
MANHOLE
COVERS

A Treasure Trove of Unique Designs
from the Streets of Japan

The Carriage Trade Press

P.O.Box 51491-Eugene,OR 97405
http://user.chollian.net/~quiltart

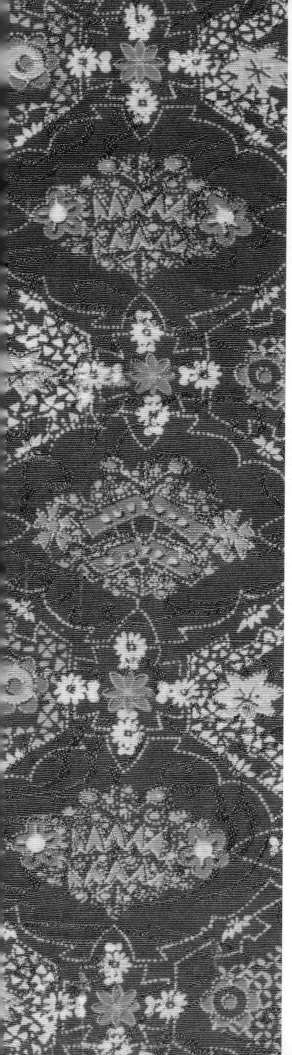

Book design by   D.D.O.D Graphic Design Agency
Editor-in-Chief   Young-In Shin
Design & Art director   Je-Hee Joh
Cover design & Technical Editor   Eun-Suk So
Color Illustrator   Hwa-Young Lee
Adderess: #4 Dong-hee B/D 566-19 Shinsa-Dong Kangnam-Gu, Seoul, Korea
Tel: 82-2-3443-4029
Email: ddod1@kmail.com

Quilting with Manhole Covers: A Treasure Trove of Unique Designs from the Streets of Japan

Copyright © 1999 by Shirley MacGregor
Published by The Carriage Trade Press
P. O. Box 51491
Eugene, Oregon 97405 USA

Library of Congress Catalog Card Number: 99-90370

ISBN: 0-9671433-5-7

Printed in Seoul, Korea
by Ulchi Gracom Ltd.
E-mail : GUNNGOOK@hitel.net

Acknowledgements

The phrase "Without the help of the following people, this book would never have been printed..." seems a bit trite, but it has taken on an entirely new meaning since beginning this project. The individuals and organizations mentioned here have all been extremely important to the creation of this book. I humbly and wholeheartedly thank all who supported this effort.

Very Special Thanks to

Douglas MacGregor, for being the most supportive and encouraging husband in the world. I never would have made it through all of this process without his constant help. Doug, I know this was difficult for you, living with me when the pressure was on, and I love you for it.

Michiko Ono, who worked tirelessly for many months gathering and interpreting information, and being a true and dedicated friend.

Nobuharu & Hiroko Ueno, our good friends, who provided language and cultural information, historical data, support and encouragement, as well as some of the finest food that Japan has to offer.

Paula Golden, of the Cabin Branch Quilters, whose tireless efforts in recruiting quilters, organizing shows, and coordinating the movement of a growing stable of manhole quilts, is greatly appreciated.

Sheila Steers and Pat Hann, sisters in a most unusual game of international catch. Their spirits are tightly woven into every page.

Joji Hayashi, Tokyo artist and friend to manhole covers everywhere, for recognizing my efforts and writing the forward to this book.

Editing and Proofreading – "Blessed are the linguistically pure..."
Glenda Beasley, *Marsha Carlton*, *Nancy Jones*, *Marsha Moldenhaur*, *Ruth Osborn*, *Sheila Steers*, and *Carol Stone*

Interpreting / Translating / Research
Akemi Narita, *Satoko Sakakibara*, *Toshi Tonon*, *Rie Devine*, and *Kazuko Gomi*

All the Quilters Whose Masterpieces Appear in this Book

Quilters in Japan
Keiko Arakawa, Hiromi Fujiwara, Yuki Fushike, Harumi Iida, Fumiko Iwasawa, Tamie Kimura, Keiko Komatsu, Hiroko Morooka, Sachiko Nagaishi, Harumi Okayama, Michiko Ono, Yuko Sakurai, Motoko Sampei, Mieko Suzuki, Haruyo Yamada, Kumiko Yamada, Michi Yamada, Kikue Yamashita for listening to me, and answering a steady stream of questions.

Technical Support
Mrs. Oobayashi for information on dying methods, and Leesa Gawlik for help with dyeing of material. Also, the *D.D.O.D Graphics Team* and *G.G. Kim*, master printer.

Community Support
To officials of the cities and towns who graciously provided reprinting rights to the manhole cover designs, informational materials, and who offered their help and understanding. Notable among them are officials of Fujisawa City, Hayama Town (*Mr. Takahashi* of the sewer department, and *Mrs. Fukuda* of the cultural committee for her enthusiasm and for displaying my manhole quilt), Yokosuka City and Zushi City.

Industry Support
Messrs. Ogiwara and *Eguchi* of Hinode Foundry, Ltd., *Messrs. Asanuma* and *Kamii* of Nihon Chuzo Casting Co., and officials of the Nagashima Foundry Co., for graciously welcoming me to their respective companies and providing valuable information.

Honorable Mention
Jackie Atkins for advice and encouragement, Ana *D'Avila* and *Heidi Tool*, for manhole photos, *Keisha Jackson*, for assisting with the initial rubbings, *Takashi* and *Masako Yokoyama, Minoru Akimoto*, Warren Elliott, *the Shimizu family*, and the entire *Zushi Highlands Running Club* for encouragement, warm friendship, generosity, and showing us the very best of Japan during our stay.

And to anyone I have left out, my most profound apology.

Outline / Index

FORWARD BY *Joji Hayashi*
THE MANHOLE COVERS

On November 12th, 1970, in Ueno Park, I took my first photograph of a manhole cover. And that was when I first became interested in them. At that time, I was studying design at Musashino University of Art, and walking around Tokyo in order to find objects with interesting designs.

At first, I paid attention only to attractive things, such as decorative buildings, billboards, items in the shop windows, traffic signs, and cars. However, I quickly tired of looking at such obvious attractions and I began to turn my eyes away from them.

I decided that there were two kinds of things in the town: flashy, attractive ones and simple "quiet" ones. As the attractive items tend to catch the eye, you are always more apt to admire them more than subtle items. However, I came to find that there were a lot of fascinating shapes and designs among a city's more mundane and practical objects.
One of these is the manhole cover. Manhole covers do not stand out; they have rather simple designs, and tend to be taken for granted and unnoticed by the average citizen. Perhaps this is because they are the gates that separate our world from the underground; doors to a mysterious world below. Their subtle designs may be to dissuade people from entering.

A manhole cover is a heavy iron object, with a rugged surface designed to prevent slipping. It is made for utility. Its varied patterns identify its reason for being, whether it be to provide access to fresh water, sewage, telecommunication or electrical wiring, or to gas lines. The various industries involved represent themselves with manhole covers in a wide variety of fascinating shapes and patterns. It is always a pleasure to find new and different covers as one moves from town to town.

At first, I was impressed mainly by the manhole cover's shiny iron face, its pleasant and durable design constantly stepped on by cars and people. But then I began to develop an interest in their history. When walking down a street, I would sometimes come across a manhole cover which was totally different from others. As they are subject to wear and damage, they are often replaced with newer models. But sometimes one will escape, one with a unique patten, different characters, or perhaps just enough wear to reflect a different era.

If you take time, you can learn a great deal from such artifacts - a date of manufacture, characters that have fallen from use, the logo of a company that no longer exists, or the name of a town which has been absorbed into a larger entity and is lost to antiquity. Take what you glean from such an investigation to the library, and you can trace the origins of the symbols that emblazon these unique tablets, and derive a deeper understanding of your surroundings.

A Brief History

The first underground utilities for fresh water and sewage incorporating manhole covers in Japan were made in the city of Yokohama between 1881 and 1887. These manholes are still in existence, but unfortunately they are missing their covers. Thus, we have no idea whether the first manhole covers were made of wood or iron.

After those in Yokohama, many manholes were constructed in various parts of Japan. The techniques employed in these early structures were introduced by the English and Americans. For example, the manhole covers in Tokyo in the early days were of American design, while those in Osaka bore a British influence. The covers, too, reflected these Anglo-American influences, although some of the cover designs began to show Japanese patterns and style.

These early manhole covers, however, were not made to decorate the streets or to attract attention, but were simple utilitarian objects.

Then, in 1978, to commemorate the Okinawa Sea Expo, a decorative manhole cover was designed portraying fish. This was probably the first cover specifically conceived to attract the attention of the public.

Since then, utility companies and municipal governments of Japan have made an effort to use decorative designs on manhole covers. City flowers, well-known tourist attractions, historic buildings and local products are all popular themes for cover designs.

In the past, manhole covers were subtle objects which were virtually unnoticed. Recently, however, these covers are beginning to attract public attention, and I must say that I am a little worried about this tendency. Unless they are well designed and conceived in good taste, the cover designs could become an embarrassment. It should be considered that once a manhole cover is placed, it might be gracing a street for fifty to one hundred years. Thus, those who select the cover designs should give very serious thought to the message they wish such designs to convey.

Although our manhole covers now have appealing designs, many Japanese citizens have failed to notice them. But now Shirley MacGregor, American quilt designer, impressed by the artistry of these covers, has begun to incorporate some of them into her work.

Manhole covers are a part of the environment of the earth. Their function might be likened to the buttons of our clothing, a pleasing compliment to the fabric upon which they rest. If their design is poor or too flashy, they will diminish the quality of the whole. I hope that more and better manhole cover designs appear in Japan. And I hope that Ms. MacGregor will create attractive quilts based upon these designs.

Joji Hayashi - July, 1997

Joji Hayashi was born in Tokyo in 1947. He graduated from the Musashi University of Art in 1972, and has published, among other works, "The Manhole Cover in Japan" (1985) and "The Manhole Cover in Europe" (1986), both by Science Publishing Co. Mr. Hayashi lives with his wife in Tokyo.

Translated by Akemi Narita

Getting The Most From This Book

This is not a "how-to" book, but rather a collection of ideas and images intended to stir your imagination. These unique designs, and their interpretation in fabric by a variety of quilters, is intended to inspire you and broaden your perspectives.

The designs which are represented here may be applied to a wide variety of quilting projects, from wall hangings to framed pictures; from throws to sampler quilts. Let the examples fire your imagination, and your creativity lead you where it will!

The methods and techniques you employ will depend upon the design you choose. If you are new to such things, try this:

- Look closely at the pictures. See how the components of the design, their flow and movement, affect you.
- Consider the color possibilities. Disregard convention, and remember that interpretations do not have to be literal.

Enlargements

The silhouettes and line drawings presented here are quite obviously restricted by the page size, and thus should be enlarged for use as patterns. Make enlargements of either or both of these representations, scaled to a desirable size. These may be used to:

- make templates based on the enlargements
- mark information or jot down ideas
- determine colors and fabrics to be used
  Note: Add seam allowances to all patterns

Copyright Notice: Please remember that the designs included in this book are copyrighted by the communities they represent. You may make artistic representations of these designs, but may not use them for any other purpose.

Techniques

Appliqué and Stencil: Pattern pieces are automatically ready when you have taken time to enlarge your pattern. Redrawing on a grid gives you the opportunity to use all or just part of the design—regardless of size—or to combine it with other designs. Remember to add seam allowances where necessary. For stenciling or hand painting make cut-outs in the enlarged pattern.

Embellishments: Beads, buckles and a variety of other items were used in many of the quilts you will find in the book. As a piece of jewelry complements a dress, such items can add a striking accent to your manhole quilt.

Trapunto: Many of the manhole cover designs are ideal for this very popular quilting method.

Quilting: If you quilt by hand, you might try a whole-cloth or sashiko (a Japanese method with large stitching and heavy thread). If you are quilting with a machine, experiment with threads of varied color and size to add depth to your design.

Treasures Underfoot

It was while jogging through the back streets of Zushi during my first autumn in Japan that I began what was to become an intimate relationship with Japanese manhole covers. At 5 AM when most people were still snug in their futons, I would take to the streets for my morning exercise. The roads were free of traffic at that hour, and manhole covers were in full view. I was immediately impressed with the intricate design the city fathers had chosen for these rather heavy objets d'art, and salted the pattern away in my mind for future reference.

As time passed, and I wandered farther afield, I noticed manhole covers with equally striking patterns representing other communities. This kept my mind in the gutter, so to speak, and whenever I arrived in an unexplored town or city, I eagerly anticipated investigating the street hardware.

I had been considering ideas for a Japanese quilt, toying with traditional themes, mainly nature, bamboo, sand and rock gardens but those manhole covers kept staring up at me, begging consideration. And eventually they won.

I chose two covers of which I was particularly fond—Hayama Town (Zushi's neighbor to the north), and Kanagawa Prefecture (the larger governmental entity of which Zushi and Hayama are part). I thought the designs would look great in silk, and began roughing out a pattern. But what would I use for a backdrop for these beautiful and symbolic tributes to the founder's craft? After all, their purpose was to cover up sewers! Should I stick with the implied theme and portray a sewage scene? That would certainly look interesting on the wall. I would just have to tiptoe around the grim truth somehow and see what developed.

Now, how to construct the cover patterns? I decided I would take the romantic route and do "rubbings", an art popular in the churches of Europe, where one uses paper or foil to lift the relief images from burial vaults. I had always wanted to do this while living in England, but never found the opportunity. It struck me that taking a rubbing from a manhole cover might satisfy this unfulfilled desire. I began my search for two relatively unblemished lids, reasonably free of dirt, rust and bird droppings. Within a few days, I had zeroed in on my targets.

With the help of a loyal friend (she had to be loyal to get roped into such a bizarre activity!) I took to the streets. After a bit of anxious dodging and weaving, and only minor disruption to local traffic, my friend and I managed to obtain two fairly accurate rubbings and return home unscathed. I then set to work on my pattern.

I transferred the designs to butcher paper and clean up the rough spots on the impressions that we had made. My next challenge was to locate the perfect material to represent the manhole covers.

After perusing my stacks of material, and checking local sources, I could find nothing that looked remotely like weathered iron. In desperation, I contacted a friend in Oregon for ideas. She sent material with the right pattern, but several shades off the desired color. This offered more promise than anything else I had encountered, so I sent for more. Meanwhile, I presented my problem to an American friend who does surface design. She suggested a combination of bleaching and painting that produced a very satisfactory effect.

Slowly, the project began to take shape. I sorted through my fabric collection for strips of silk, while keeping an eye out for dissectable *kimono* at local rummage sales. As the weeks passed, students and friends generously donated scraps. Soon, my small studio was amply adorned with a few hundred swatches awaiting assignment.

I cut out the butcher paper patterns to form a stencil. I then transferred the template pattern to my manhole cloth, cutting an appliqué for each cover.

The central theme for the background of the quilt became a river meandering diagonally from the top to the bottom of the quilt. The surrounding "land," made up of horizontally-placed strips of silk, was rather plain and uncluttered at its upper reaches, but became more complex as it descended. In similar fashion, the river became more "eventful" as it flowed into the symbolic population area. I appliqued the manhole cover designs on this backdrop with Hayama on the bottom left, among the "urban silks," and Kanagawa in a more lofty position (due to its stature as prefecture) to the northeast.

This was a particularly labor-intensive project, both in planning and execution, and required nearly two years of reasonably consistent work to complete.
But the effort provided some unique and fascinating experiences that I shall never forget.

While making the quilt, I became so taken with manhole cover designs that I was unable to let the subject rest. I began to think that I had been chosen by a local sewer spirit for a special mission: to make the Japanese aware of the iron gems that adorned their streets. Meanwhile, the idea of presenting the designs to quilters everywhere grew stronger with the passage of time. A book, perhaps?

Here were unique and original designs with fascinating stories to tell. A veritable treasure trove of artistic expression was lying in the streets of Japan, awaiting discovery! But when I began to ponder the implications of producing a book on the subject, the whole idea seemed truly daunting.

My first consideration was to determine if there were enough manhole designs in Japan to warrant the effort. I had seen a half dozen or so in my local area, but had no idea how widespread the practice of manhole decoration might be. Perhaps it was a phenomenon limited to the area in which I lived.

Next, would there be a market for such a book? I certainly thought the cover designs were great, but would anyone else? After all, it is a peculiar medium which admittedly carries some rather unsavory connotations.

In addition to these concerns, getting permission to use copyrighted designs posed multiple problems. I presumed that each town or city would hold the rights to its particular cover design, and that I would have to approach each to obtain permission for their use. Being a female "gaijin" (foreigner), with very limited language skills, this would be no small task. Communicating my bizarre idea to bureaucrats in a number of Japanese communities seemed just a bit ambitious.

Another hurdle would be to obtain clear, well-defined images of the cover designs. I could picture myself dashing into busy streets with a basket of cleaning materials and a camera. Japanese drivers are patient and polite, but there are limits.

I decided to carry the fantasy just a little further, and began an informal "market survey." I asked my Japanese quilting students and several friends what they thought of their local manhole covers. That is when I made the startling discovery that virtually no one had ever noticed them! Invariably, my questions on the subject were met with blank stares and puzzled responses. The more people I asked, more this sad fact was borne out. When I introduced them to these elegant iron artifacts, however, they seemed truly delighted. The quilters thought that the designs would, indeed, make interesting quilt patterns, and this encouraged me to continue.

Testing the Waters

The next area of concern was feasibility. I had to determine what was out there and how accessible it was. For this I asked the help of two bilingual Japanese friends, and discussed the matter with them at length. Although my two confidantes thought I was nuts (and perhaps still do!), they found the project fascinating, and were more than willing to lend a hand.

Our plan of action was to make a few fact-finding visits to administrative offices of communities in our immediate area. First would be Zushi, the city in which I lived, followed by the neighboring cities of Fujisawa, Yokosuka and Hayama.

There is a hierarchy in a Japanese municipal office that only a bureaucrat could love. When seeking information, one is obliged to begin with the most junior official on the administrative ladder and progress slowly along, explaining the nature of one's request to each individual in his turn. So, office by office, we carefully worked our way through the pecking order explaining what we were up to. Even with the ladies carefully laying out the situation in Japanese, our request was understandably difficult to convey. To their credit, the officials to whom we spoke were always patient and agreeable, although often puzzled. They told us the origins of their designs, how and when they came into existence, and often a bit about their sewage and water systems. They also informed us that if we wished to use the designs, we would have to make formal requests in writing, stating how we intended to use them.

Major deliberations ensued as my astute colleagues pains-takingly drafted a letter sure to win the hearts and minds of the city fathers of the four target communities. It was a fascinating lesson in cultural difference (and deference, if you will). I have never seen so much care and consideration go into such a small letter! But I was assured that such attention to detail could easily mean the difference between success and failure.

At this point I began to think that visiting a manhole cover manufacturer wouldn't be a bad idea. With a few leads from the municipal offices we had visited, I was able to locate two foun-dries in the Yokohama area, Nihon Chuzo and Hinode, Ltd., and made appointments to call on them.

We were graciously received by foundry officials, again with a great deal of curiosity. Our hosts were quite enthusiastic about their products and provided us interesting background information on a wide variety of topics, from history to some of the technical aspects in the casting process. I learned that the copyrights I was seeking were indeed held by the individual communities, so my hopes of obtaining permission to use a number of designs from one source were dashed. The good news was that the foundries had catalogs of their manhole covers, and they generously presented me with free copies. The catalogs set my mind at ease on at least one issue: There was certainly no shortage of artistically-rendered manhole covers in Japan. The number and variety surpassed my wildest expectations.

Now the next challenge—could I obtain permission from the various cities and towns to use their designs? Zushi and Yokosuka had by this time granted their approval, which was extremely encouraging and helpful as I set about the next stage in my quest.

My colleagues carefully drafted a second form letter stating my request for use of the designs. This time it was more persuasive, in that two notable municipalities had already tendered their consent. It must have worked, as over the next several weeks we received positive replies to a clear majority of our requests. Each new day brought another large envelope or two with copies of the coveted designs, along with booklets listing community services and amenities. Most importantly, included in each package was permission to use the design. Another bridge crossed, and more adventures ahead!

Treasures Underfoot—the inspiration for this book—is probably the first quilt to be based on manhole cover designs. The cover to the lower left is that of Hayama Town, neighboring community to Zushi, where I lived. In the upper right of the quilt is the cover design of Kanagawa Prefecture, of which Hayama and Zushi are part.

The water represents the cleansed sewer water as it flows toward the sea.

Treasures Underfoot received a first place at the 1997 Pacific International Quilt Festival in Santa Clara, CA.

On the following pages are pictures of the two covers whose designs are represented in the quilt.

Hayama Town

Four hundred citizens of Hayama entered designs in a competition to select a cover design. The winning design artfully represents all of the town's symbols. Hayama's flower is the azalea, its bird is the nightingale, and its tree, the black pine. The sailboat, although fitting to any coastal town, is significant in that Hayama was first to have a yacht club.

Hayama Town

This is the model for the Hayama cover represented in the quilt, *"Treasures Underfoot,"* shown on the previous page.

Kanagawa Prefecture

The cover below is that of Kanagawa Prefecture. In Japan, a prefecture is a governmental entity which lies somewhere between an American county and a state.

The seat of government of Kanagawa is Yokohama, Japan's most important port city, and gateway to the West. In 1853, Commodore Matthew Perry of the US Navy sailed brazenly into this port with his notorious "Black Ships" to tender a rather forceful "invitation" to the Japanese government to join United States in trade.

A few kilometers to the south of Yokohama is the city of Yokosuka, a thriving coastal community and home port of the United States 7th Fleet, which constitutes America's most significant military presence in Asia.

The city of Kamakura, second only in historical significance to Kyoto, and birthplace of Japanese Zen Buddhism, is located in the prefecture.

Hayama Town, whose cover design is also featured in these pages, graces Kanagawa's coastline, and is the location of the emperor's summer palace.

Nestled snugly between Kamakura and Hayama is the charming city of Zushi, where I lived for four years.

綾瀬 あやせ

Ayase City

Beginning as an agricultural community on the outskirts of metropolitan Tokyo, the area developed in a random fashion until its incorporation in 1978.

Amidst increasing urbanization and industrial development, the city fathers are attempting to achieve a balance among manufacturing, agricultural and environmental interests. Fairs, festivals, and promotion of local agricultural products are helping to instill a rural atmosphere in the community.

Elaine Myers   *"Shadows of Spring Leaves"*
Manassas, Virginia
Size: 34" x 30"
Photo: Ed Barr

"My initial vision of the leaves was a flurry of autumn colors, but as I looked through my fabrics, the very green silk kept speaking to me, and I began to think in terms of spring green leaves on a black background." But when I came across the textured black fabric, the lines in it looked so much like the veins in the leaves, that I reversed the two colors, and loved the effect!"

Ayase's two manhole cover designs are inspired by the city's flower (the rose) and its tree (the Japanese maple).

藤野町

Fujino Town

Fujino Town is located on lake Sagami in the extreme northern part of Kanagawa Prefecture. Its natural setting has attracted a number of artists over the years, and there are many sculptures to be seen throughout the town. Meijinomori Takao Quasi National Park and Mount Jinba are nearby, and offer popular hiking trails.

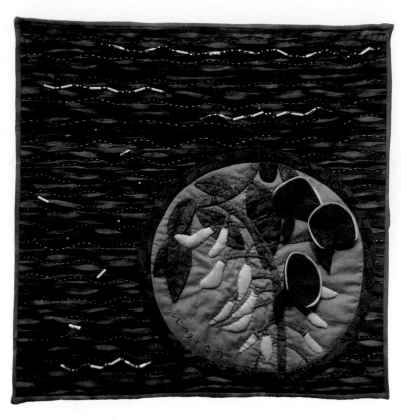

"I decided that since the quilt was based on a Japanese manhole cover, I would try writing a Haiku to go along with it. It has the 5-7-5 (syllable) pattern, although I think in traditional Haiku the theme relates to the seasons, but this one was close."

Lifegiving water
Sparkles in the sun as the
Sweet Pea vine extends. - Steele

"The wall hanging is a combination of hand and machine applique, machine quilting and Sashiko. The Sashiko is not a traditional pattern but follows the lines of the background fabric representing water. The stitches of rayon floss are longer than a quilting stitch and go through only the top and batting. The beads remind me of stones glistening in a stream."

Barbara Steele   *"Sweet Pea in the Sun"*
Woodbridge, Virginia
Size: approx.16" diameter
Photo: Ed Barr

Karen Harmony
"We All Live Downstream"
Vida, Oregon
Size: 35" x 47.5"
Photo: Karen Harmony

"I have spent my entire life on the banks of rivers. Growing up on the levees of the Mississippi River in New Orleans, I later moved to the Kings River watershed in the Arkansas Ozark Mountains. I now live on the banks of the McKenzie River in the Oregon Cascade Mountains. It has always been clear to me that we do indeed all live downstream, and that it is imperative that we maintain the cleanliness and health of the water on Planet Earth."

The town's manhole cover features the wisteria, which is the town flower.

Linda Mossey   *"Osuri"*
Ohyabe, Japan
Quilt size: 25" diameter
Photo: Shirley MacGregor

"I was drawn to the pine tree *matsu* pattern. I liked the way the branches were a bit off center... [and] the light/dark pattern design that gave an impression of needles.... I wanted to make the size about the same as the manhole cover in real life. It... challenged me to open my eyes and see the possibility of design in the simple things around me...."

The two Fujisawa manhole covers that appear in this book depict the city flower (wisteria) and its tree (the pine).

Fujisawa City
Manhole Covers

Fukui City

Fukui is a coastal community situated near the geographical center of Japan. It is a very old city, and was a feudal capital in the 15th century. Fukui has been totally destroyed two times in recent history, first by bombing raids during WWII, and again by a powerful earthquake in 1948.

福井市

Hakodate City

函館市

An important city in southern Hokkaido, Hakodate rose to prominence in the mid-1800's as a result of a trade treaty inspired by American Commodore Matthew Perry. Hakodate was selected, along with Yokohama and Nagasaki, to become a port for international trade. From that point, the city came under strong western influence, which can still be seen today. An impressive "Port Festival" is held during the first week of August each year to commemorate this opening of trade with the west.

Nancy Jones   *"Three's A Charm"*
Woodbridge, Virginia
Size : 21" diameter
Photo : Ed Barr

"I chose this design because I have 3 daughters, and the tentacles remind me of their wild hair. If you look closely, I have sewn each of the girls names into each of the squid (Carol Ann, Sarah Louise and Emily)."

The manhole cover design features a squid, symbolic of the city's fishing industry.

Hasuda City

Hasuda City is located about 40 Km northwest of metropolitan Tokyo in eastern Saitama Prefecture. Saitama boasts the fairest weather in all of Japan, which makes agriculture an important part of its economy. Hasuda City is a famous pear growing area. The city is currently seeking a "sister city" relationship with a community in Oregon or Washington.

蓮田

Bunnie Jordan
"Lotus Blossom"
Vienna, Virginia
Size: 24" x 29"
Photo: Bunnie Jordan

"This piece is worked in the traditional style of a Japanese scroll, marked by the unequal top and bottom borders. The hanging ribbons are another feature of the traditional scroll. The lotus blossom is a symbol of purity and beauty since it can bloom even in the mud. It also symbolizes the highest level of human development and understanding."

Several water lilies grace Hasuda's manhole cover

Izumiotsu City

"Izumiotsu is like a gemstone— small, yet packed with dazzling beauty...." So state the city fathers of this community on Osaka Bay. Although it rests in the shadow of Osaka City's metropolitan complex, it retains a measure of individuality and a strong sense of pride in its ancient heritage.

During the Edo period, Izumiotsu emerged as a major producer of cotton. It has since become a major textile center specializing in the manufacture of knitwear and blankets.

泉大津市

Margaret (Marty) Moon
"A Mother and Her Baby"
Culpepper, Virginia
Size: 29" x 55"
Photo: Margaret Moon

"When I saw the manhole covers at the Cabin Branch Quilt Show in Woodbridge, VA in October, 1998, I was fascinated with them to say the least....The wheels started turning instantly and I could visualize my mama sheep and lamb in fabric."

"My friends have had a good chuckle over my antics, but I actually stopped the car one day as I was driving through a shopping center parking lot and measured a manhole cover."

"Sheep are very peaceful animals and I believe that this is reflected in my quilt. Not a person that has seen my sheep as I've worked on it has been able to resist reaching out to touch. They look as if they can be petted."

Sheep adorn Izumiotsu's manhole cover, symbolizing its textile industry.

Kaita Town

Just 10 km east of the city of Hiroshima, Kaita shared the grim realities of nuclear devastation with its larger neighbor. Today, Kaita is a growing community looking toward a bright future.

海田町

Mary Beth Wiesner   *"Sunflower at Twilight"*
Woodbridge, Virginia
Size : Size: 26" x 26"
Photo : Ed Barr

"...I loved the boldness of the flowers. The checkerboard flower centers were so cheerful and the polka dots in the background provided just the right touch of whimsy. I used about 100 orchid-colored wooden beads for the polka dots. Any flowers in my garden are always covered with bugs, so I though I should add some to my sunflowers."

Kaita Town's manhole cover design features sun flowers, which reflect the hopes and dreams of its citizens for a better life.

Kamaishi City

Kamaishi is located in Rikuchu Coast National Park in Iwate Prefecture. With a long tradition as a fishing community, Kamaishi is also a center for iron and steel production, and has a sizable tourist industry.

A fearsome tiger adorns the Kamaishi manhole cover. Long ago, a man by the name of Hehi governed the area. When Hehi's third son became a warrior, legend has it that he danced with a stuffed tiger to symbolize his bravery. This became a tradition followed by other young warriors.

かまいし

Haruko Obayashi
Zushi, Japan
Quilted by Shirley MacGregor
Photos: Shirley MacGregor

"Kamaishi City I"
(Size:14 x 14" Bingata quilt)

The white background was made using a traditional stenciling method called Bingata. This is an old traditional art form in Okinawa, Japan. The pigments come from natural dyes made from leaves, trees and flowers. The darker shades provide accent to the lighter color, such as the teeth of the tiger.

"Kamaishi City II"
(Size:14" x 14" Aisome quilt)

The tiger is stenciled on a linen background using a method called Aisome. This is an ancient art form that incorporates colors made from indigo leaves. The indigo dye looks like blue, but is made of many colors; red, yellow, brown, green and of course blue. Aisome blue is very rich because it diffuses and reflects light.

The tiger on the manhole cover design represents the spirit and bravery of the people of Kamaishi.

Makubetsu City

Hokkaido Prefecture has four very distinct seasons, all highly regarded by the citizens of Makubetsu City. With spring come the cherry blossoms, with summer, the song birds, with the autumn, salmon swell the local rivers. And as winter approaches, the beloved swans return to the area.

まくべつ

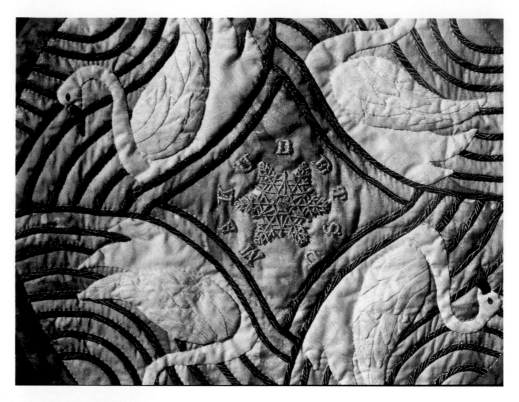

Karen S. Walker   *"Don't Fence Me In"*
Warrenton, Virginia
Size:19" X 33"
Photo:Karen S. Walker

"Each swan [has] a separate wing, with 17 feathers---arrrgh!-- on each. My thought with each feather was; why, why, can't I just do something simple for a change!"

"The center features an embroidered snowflake and lettering in gold metallic thread. The quilting design, fences, is from a sashiko book. I liked the design and decided it was appropriate to name the quilt 'Don't Fence Me In'."

Four swans (the city's bird) are the dominant feature of the Makubetsu cover design. A snowflake in the center of the design signifies the winter season that brings these graceful creatures each year.

宮崎市

Miyazaki City

Miyazaki City, capital of the prefecture that bears the same name, is located on the eastern coast of Kyushu. The Nihonshoki—one of Japan's oldest historical documents—describes the area around Miyazaki as "the cradle of Japanese civilization." According to Shinto legend, it is here that Jummu, the semi-mythical first emperor of Japan was born. Beyond the legend, Miyazaki has a rich historical heritage that reaches well back into prehistory.

Cathy Sperry
"Iris in the Road"
Anaheim Hills, California
Quilt Size : 22" diameter
Photo : Ed Barr

"*'The Iris in the Road'* is my first attempt at interpreting a realistic object. It is also my first circular quilt and I found that to be challenging in itself, just keeping it ROUND! When I first saw the black and white drawing....I immediately thought of the Japanese iris that grow in my front yard. The morning sun shines on them in such a way that the leaves almost look translucent."

Three iris blossoms (the city's flower) provide the theme for Miyazaki City's manhole cover, with the city symbol in the center.

Morioka City

Morioka, a city of 235,000, is the capital of Iwate Prefecture in northeastern Honshu. It was a castle town in the early Edo period, ruled by the Nambu clan. Each year in early August, the city celebrates the Sansa Odori festival, dating back 170 years. The dance procession numbers some 20,000 participants.

盛岡市

帯広市

Obihiro City

Obihiro City is situated in the agricultural heartland of Hokkaido, in the north of Japan. Each year, in late January, to make the best of the bitter cold weather that prevails during the long winter season, the city plays host to the Obihiro Ice Festival. Here masters of the art gather to delight visitors with their creations.

Odawara City

Odawara is located in Kanagawa Prefecture at the main entrance to the Fuji Hakone Izu National Park, an area of great natural beauty.

In the early 17th century, Odawara was an important stop along the road between Edo (Tokyo) and Kyoto. The city's noble past is reflected in its impressive castle, and the beautiful Daiyuzan Saijoji Temple, set in a grove of massive 400-500-year-old cedars.

小田原市

Oguni Town

小国町

Oguni Town rests in a basin surrounded by lovely mountains in the center of Niigata Prefecture, 80 kilometers from Niigata City. Each winter, Oguni receives between 150 and 200 centimeters of snow. The name Oguni means "small country" in Japanese, and in its isolation, it appears to be just that.

Oguni Washi, handmade Japanese paper, is famous throughout the country, and has been designated as an "intangible cultural asset" by the government.

Paula Golden
Woodbridge, Virginia
Size: 29" x 29"
Photo: Ed Barr

"The design on the Oguni Town manhole cover reminded me of the beautiful peonies that bloom in my garden during the month of May. Creating a textured background for the flowers is symbolic of the many facets of the lives we live."

The tsubaki, or snow camellia, is pictured on Oguni's manhole cover.
The tree has a large, white or light pink flower, and also represents the
pretty women of the northern part of Japan.

Ojiya City

Ojiya City rests on the banks of Japan's longest river, the Shinano, in the mountainous "snow country" of Niigata Prefecture. The city has long been known for the weaving of Ojiya Chijimi, a crinkled linen fabric, and its "swimming jewels," Nishiki-goi, a particularly beautiful breed of koi (or carp). The Ojiya area is the setting for "Snow Country," a famous novel by Yasunari Kawabata.

おぢや

Mary Magneson
"Three Koi"
Fredericksburg, Virginia
Size: 25 1/2" diameter
Photo: Ed Barr

"I was intrigued by the idea of using a design on something as basic as a manhole cover. I chose Ojiya City because of the 'fancy carp' or koi fish. Several years ago I was asked to design a flag or banner with koi on it. Since that time I have fallen in love with the simple beauty of these creatures. I strove for a literal interpretation of this cover to show the simplicity."

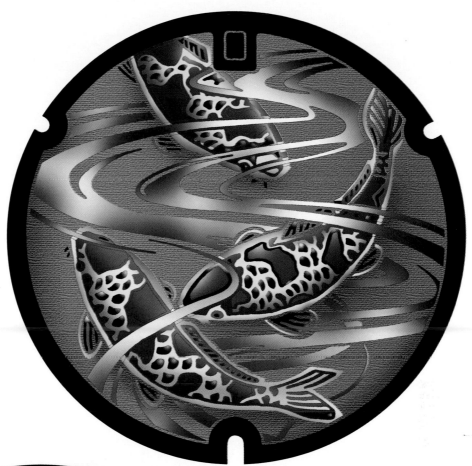

One of Ojiya's manhole cover designs is its city flower, the narcissus, chosen as a harbinger of spring. Another cover depicts three Nishiki-goi swimming in the river.

Ozu Town

In the early spring, some 400,000 red, white and pink azaleas burst into bloom and dramatically announce the end of the winter season to the citizens of Ozu Town.

Ozu is located in Kumamoto Prefecture on the island of Kyushu. Kumamoto was once home to Musasi Miyamoto, one of the more colorful characters of Japanese history.

A man of varied talents, Miyamoto was a student of Zen Buddhist philosophy, an author, a master of the Japanese tea ceremony, and a teacher of Chinese black-ink painting. But he is perhaps most noted as a respected sword master and tactician, having created the niten'echeryu sword-fighting style (using swords in both hands, equally).

大津

おおづ おすい

Ann Weaver
"Spring Blossom"
Roanoke, Virginia
Size: 24.5" diameter
Photo: Ed Barr

"Memories of spring blossoms in Japan are brought to life in this manhole cover design."

Ozu Town's cover design shows three azaleas on a dotted background.

Carolyn Jensen *"Third Time's a Charm"*
Yokosuka, Japan
Size: 42 1/2" x 42 1/2"
Photo: Shirley MacGregor

"I tried to arrange the colors of the many hydrangeas we see here in Japan from light to dark on the blossom head. The name of this quilt comes from the three different sets of leaves I appliqued to the quilt top."

Sagamihara's cover design depicts the city flower, the hydrangea.

Pat Hann
"Maple River"
Ipswitch, England
Size: 21" diameter
Photo: Shirley MacGregor

"Manhole, manhole, manhole—what Shirley?... Magically the manholes appeared over the internet, we blew them up, and I chose the most realistic one to try and do a silk painting of. I blew it up on the photocopier to the size of the wall-quilt-to-be, and then got out my silk paints."

This particular design was chosen by the mayor of Sango to bring to mind a poem (shown on page 95) inscribed in the 6th century Man'yoshu, which is the oldest known book of Japanese poetry.

Sannan Town

Sannan Town is a very old community situated in a fertile river valley near Kobe, in Hyogo Prefecture. Its name signifies its location on the south side of the Chugoku mountain range.

The importance of old shrines and temples in the area has been brought into focus by Murakame Eiichi, a notable citizen of Sannan town, who has kept the ancient art of constructing and repairing these sacred structures alive in the hearts and minds of his fellow citizens.

Fearing that the secrets of his unique trade would be lost to future generations, Eiichi established an institute in the town where his students learn this age-old craft.

Patsy Monk
"Flower Kaleidoscope"
Virginia Beach, Virginia
Size : 26" diameter
Photo : Ed Barr

"When I saw this design I immediately thought of the beautiful chrysanthemums that glow in the fall sunlight. The chrysanthemum means cheerfulness under adversity."

The chrysanthemum and the pine–Sannan's flower and tree–are the components of its manhole cover design, which was the inspiration of Ms. Mayumi Segawa, a town official.

下関市

Shimonoseki City

Shimonoseki is the capital of Yamaguchi Prefecture, and is located a the southwestern tip of the island of Honshu. A city of 270,000 it is known for the very tasty, but potentially lethal, delicacy *fugu*, or blowfish. Fugu must be prepared by licensed chefs as it contains a very potent poison.

Laura Chapman *"Hootie and Company"*
Charleston, South Carolina
Size : 26.5" x 26.5"
Photo : Ed Barr

"The whimsical nature of this design prompted me to choose bright colors and shining embellishments. The circular designs resemble bubbles, and thus I chose iridescent colors and threads. Hootie, playfully encircles his blowfish friend, who takes center stage."

Shimonoseki has two manhole covers, both depicting the incomparable fugu.

田尻町

Tajiri Town

A coastal community with beautiful white sandy beaches, Tajiri Town is just a stone's throw from Osaka. Tajiri is the home of the new Kansai International Airport, yet still clings to its agricultural heritage. The area is a major producer of onions.

Toyoake City

Toyoake City is a thriving community located just a few kilometers southeast of Nagoya, in Aichi Prefecture. The city has a rich cultural heritage which is shared through colorful festivals throughout the year.

Toyoake is also the site of the battle of Okehazama wherein one Yoshimoto Imagawa, leading a 25,000-man army bent on conquering the city of Kyoto, was defeated by a force of 3,000 led by Nobunaga Oda.

豊
明

The cover design, created by Mr. Mituyosi Hori, was chosen from a field of 1,008. It depicts the city's flower and tree, the sunflower and the Keyaki.

Uchinada Town

Uchinada is situated along the coast of Ichikawa prefecture between Fukui and Kanazawa in southeastern Honshu. Because of its coastal location, sand dunes are plentiful in the town.

Uchinada's economic base centers around agriculture and textiles.

内
灘
町

道水下町灘内

Terry Schnitger
Sante Fe, New Mexico
Size: 27" diameter
Photo: Shirley MacGregor

"I was able to share [the quilts] development with my Japanese and American friends.... I chose the colors of the sea to reflect my feeling for that part of Japan while living along the seaside in Kamoi. The seagull has significant meaning in my life in Japan as I lived each day in their company."

The community's manhole cover design shows a seagull flying over rippling dunes, carrying hopes of harmony and prosperity in years to come.

Yamanakako Village

Yamanakako Village sits on the shores of Lake Yamanaka, at the foot of majestic Mt. Fuji. Just an hour and a half from Tokyo, it is an important tourist area. Each year in the spring, the community hosts the Yamanakako Marathon, which is quite popular with the Zushi Highlands Running Club.

山中湖村

やまなかこ　おすい

Barbara Scharf
Woodbridge, Virginia
Size: 20" diameter
Photo: Barbara Scharf

"….when I saw the copy of this manhole cover, I was drawn to it. When I look at this piece, I am reminded of what it was like to live in the Pacific Northwest (on a clear day!)."

126

Yamanakako's manhole cover design pictures a family of swans on the lake, with Mt. Fuji looming in the background.

Zushi City

As Zushi was our home for the four years we spent in Japan, it holds a special place in our hearts, as do the many friends that we made during our stay.

Although it has a sizable population, which swells to unsettling proportions during the tourist season, this city on picturesque Sagami Bay is comfortable and well-balanced, and maintains a strong sense of community.

But there is a great deal more to this peaceful and scenic resort city. Zushi's colorful past is closely tied to that of Kamakura, its neighbor to the north. It was during the Kamakura period of Japanese history that the samurai held sway over the land. Ascend the steeply-rising hills that surround Zushi and you will find ancient roads once traveled by these feudal knights on their way to and from the former capital.

逗子市

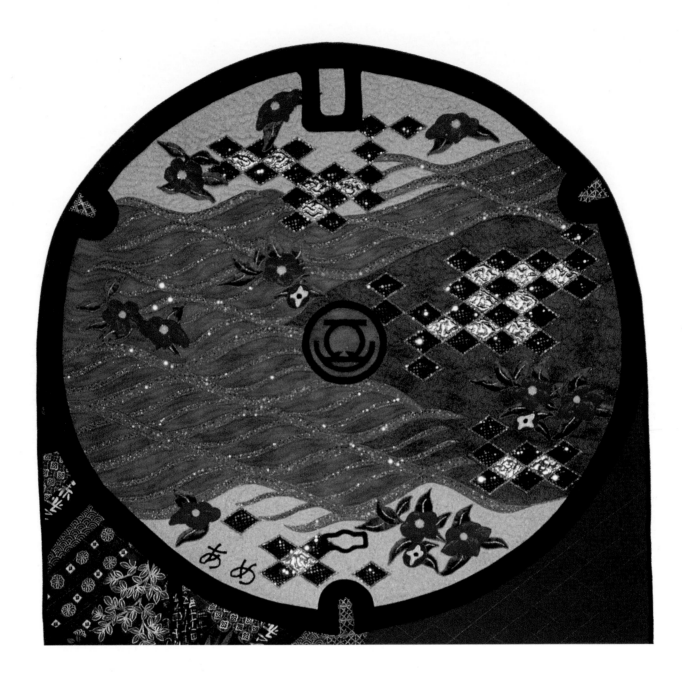

Cynthia Sisler Simms
Woodbridge, Virginia
Size: 47.5" x 47 "
Photo: Paula Golden

"When I first saw the manhole cover for Zushi City, I knew that it had to be the one for me.... I used cottons for the backgrounds of sand, water and land. And for the main designs, I used tissue lamés, crushed velour and polyester with sequins, along with metallic threads in a satin stitch to enhance those fabrics."

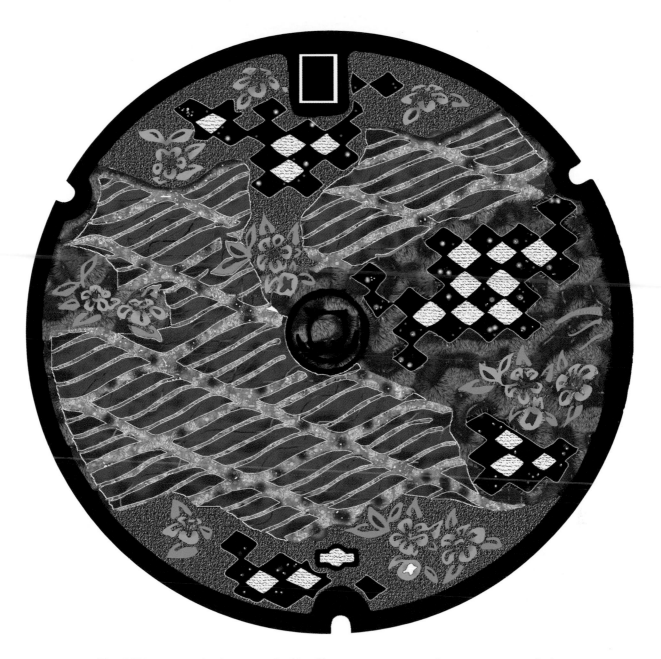

Zushi's cover design symbolically represents various aspects of the community. The dominant feature is the interlocking wave pattern that represents the waters of Sagami Bay. Groups of diamonds are interspersed among these patterns to signify population areas, and the city's flower–the camellia–appears throughout the design to suggest the natural beauty of the area.

BIBLIOGRAPHY

Hayashi, Joji, *Manhole Covers in Japan*, Tokyo: Saientistu-sha, 1984

Hayashi, Joji, *Manhole Covers in Europe,* Tokyo: Saientistu-sha, 1986

Rojyo no Monsho. Tokyo: Suido Sangyo Shinbun-sha, 1992

Rojyo no Monsho. Tokyo: Suido Sangyo Shinbun-sha, 1988

Rojyo no Monsho. Tokyo: Suido Sangyo Shinbun-sha, 1983

REFERENCES

Dietrich, Mimi and Roxi Eppler. *The Easy Art of Applique*. Washington: That Patchwork Place, Inc. 1997

Hargrave, Harriet. *Mastering Machine Applique*. California: C & T Publishing, 1990

Horton. *Fabric Makes the Quilt*. California: C & T Publishing, 1995

Kimball, Jeana. *Loving Stitches*. Washington: That Patchwork Place, Inc. 1992

Lehman, Libby. *Threadplay with Libby Lehman*. Washington: That Patchwork Place, Inc. 1997

Noble, Maurine. *Machine Quilting Made Easy*. Washington: That Patchwork Place, Inc. 1996

Simmons, Judy. *Machine Needlelace and Other Embellishment Techniques*. Washington: That Patchwork Place, Inc. 1997

Sienkiewicz, Elly. *Applique 12 Easy Ways!*. California: C & T Publishing

9. THIRD TIME'S A CHARM
Sagamehara City
Carolyn Jensen
Yokosuka, Japan

10. THREE'S A CHARM
Hakodate City
Nancy Daprile Jones
Woodbridge, Virginia

11. CALLA LILIES
Hirokami City
Bunnie Jordan
Vienna, Virginia

12. LOTUS BLOSSOM
Hasuda City
Bunnie Jordan
Vienna, Virginia

13. TREASURES UNDERFOOT
Kanagawa Prefecture and Hayama Town
Shirley MacGregor
Seoul, Korea

14. THREE KOI
Ojiya City
Mary Magneson
Fredricksburg, Virginia

15. TOYOAKE CITY
Mary Magneson
Fredricksburg, Virginia

16. FLOWER KALEIDOSCOPE
Sannan Town
Patsy Monk
Virginia Beach, Virginia

17. A MOTHER AND HER BABY
Izumiotsu City
Margaret (Marty) Moon
Culpepper, Virginia

18. OSURI
Fujisawa City
Linda Mossey
Manassas, Virginia

19. SHADOWS OF SPRING LEAVES
Ayase City
Elaine Myers
Manassas, Virginia

20. SPRINGTIME FUJISAWA
Fujisawa
Carole Nicholas
Oakton, Virginia

21. KAMAISHI CITY I AND II
Haruko Obayashi
Zushi, Japan
Both pieces quilted with
Japanese Sashiko by
Shirley MacGregor

22. A YAMANKAKO VILLAGE
Barbara Scharf
Woodbridge, Virginia

23. UCHINADA
Uchinada City
Terry Schnitger
Sante Fe, New Mexico

24. IRIS ENTWINED
Morioka City (Tonan)
Judy Sheldon
Woodbridge, Virginia

25. ZUSHI CITY
Cynthia Sisler Simms
Woodbridge, Virginia

26. COMMON THREADS
Hinode Town
Roz Skryzpek
Woodbridge, Virginia

27. TOKYO ROADS
Tokyo
Louise Rickabaugh Smith
Eugene, Oregon

28. IRIS IN THE ROAD
Miyazaki City
Cathy Sperry
Anaheim Hills, California

29. SWEET PEA IN THE SUN
Fnjino Town
Barbara DiPietro Steele
Woodbridge, Virginia

30. FISH LADDERS
Odawara City
Sheila Steers
Eugene, Oregon

31. LILIES OF OBIHIRO
Obihiro City
Sheila Steers
Eugene, Oregon

32. JAPANESE FIRE CALL
Yokosuka City
Marion Stein
Woodbridge, Virginia

33. NISHIHARIMA-KAIGAN
Jenny Terry
Ipswitch, England

34. THE ROSE REMEMBERS
Ayase City
Barbara Tricarico
Vienna, Virginia

35. DON'T FENCE ME IN
Makubetsu Town
Karen S. Walker
Warrenton, Virginia

36. SPRING BLOSSOM
Ozu Town
Ann Weaver
Roanoke, Virginia

37. SUNFLOWERS
Kaita Town
Beth Weisner
Woodbridge, Virginia

38. KOTA TOWN COVER
Terri Willet
Fairfax, Virginia

Mission statement: "To enrich the lives of people of all ages, backgrounds, and cultures through the celebration of, education about, and preservation of quilters and quiltmaking."

The Rocky Mountain Quilt Museum
1111 Washington Ave., Golden, CO
303-277-0377 RMQM @ att.net

SCFD
Scientific & Cultural
Facilities District

Manhole Cover Quilts
Gallery II
Exhibit Development: Shirley MacGregor
Exhibit Sponsor: City of Golden

Shirley MacGregor first discovered the art of Japanese Manhole covers while living in Zushi, Japan where she lived until 1997. As time went on she discovered that virtually every city and town had it it own designs that reflected one or more aspect of the community. Some portray significant historical event, others offer symbols of important local industries or agricultural products. Yet despite the wide range of images and styles the covers share adistinct graphic quality which seemed made to be translated into a quilt. Shirley's piece *Treasures Underfoot* would become the first manhole cover quilt. As she worked on her own quilt Shirley became so entranced by the subject that she began to consider whether it would be possible to develop a book about the use of manhole covers as quilt patterns. Working with quilters all over the world Shirley organized the publication of her book *Quilting With Manhole Covers* and the creation of the thirty eight quilts in this exhibit. The Rocky Mountain Quilt Museum is thrilled to bring this unique exhibit to Colorado for your enjoyment.

1. JOURNEY TO THE ORIENT
Yamagata City
Kris Bishop
Woodbridge, Virginia

2. THUNDERBIRDS
Fukui City
Kris Bishop
Woodbridge, Virginia

3. TAMANEGI
Tajire Town
Beth Bohara
Woodbridge, Virginia

4. WOOTIE AND COMPANY
Shimonoseki City
Laura Chapman
Charleston, South Carolina

5. OGUNI TOWN
Paula Golden
Woodbridge, Virginia

6. THISTLE
Toyama City
Iris Graves
Woodbridge, Virginia

7. SANGO TOWN
Pat Hann
Ipswitch, England

8. WE ALL LIVE DOWNSTREAM
Fujino Town
Karen Harmony
Vida, Oregon

To Move Forward: Look Backwards
Connie Tiegel
Atherton, CA

"History informs the future. Lessons are learned by studying the past. Often clues are hidden, information is lost in the passing time forcing modern interpretation of the past. What will future generations say about our century? What role do quilts have in recording historic events? In order to move forward we must look back."

Horizons III: Corona
Carol Ray Watkins
Boulder, CO

"As human beings we face a powerful imperative to explore or *journey*. Exploration is both an internal and external process. Specifically in terms of this quilt… It evolved as a result of responding to the warmth of the sun, the universal symbol of renewal."

Winner's Circle
Louisa L. Smith
Loveland, CO

"I started my journey into the new millennium by stretching the tradition… Giving myself permission to "go outside the lines" and discovering limitless possibilities and the liberated feeling that comes from taking advantage of them."

Victoriana
Sheila Groman
Sun City West, AZ

"Interest in crazy quilts wanes then resurfaces it doesn't disappear for long."

We are Columbine
Jeananne Wright
Longmont, CO

"As we enter the next century, it is important to remember that as individuals and as a caring nation we can make a difference for the safety and welfare of our school children. Being a teacher in Jefferson County Public Schools at the time, the Columbine tragedy touched me deeply and it seemed natural for me to not only express my grief, but also my hopes for a safer future in fabric and stitches."

Light-ning Up
Pat Moore
Arvada, CO

"Reflecting on the theme Odyssey 2000- I thought about the past and the journey of my life. I want to lighten up my life and make my next years a time of joy and the freedom to do what is really meaningful to me."

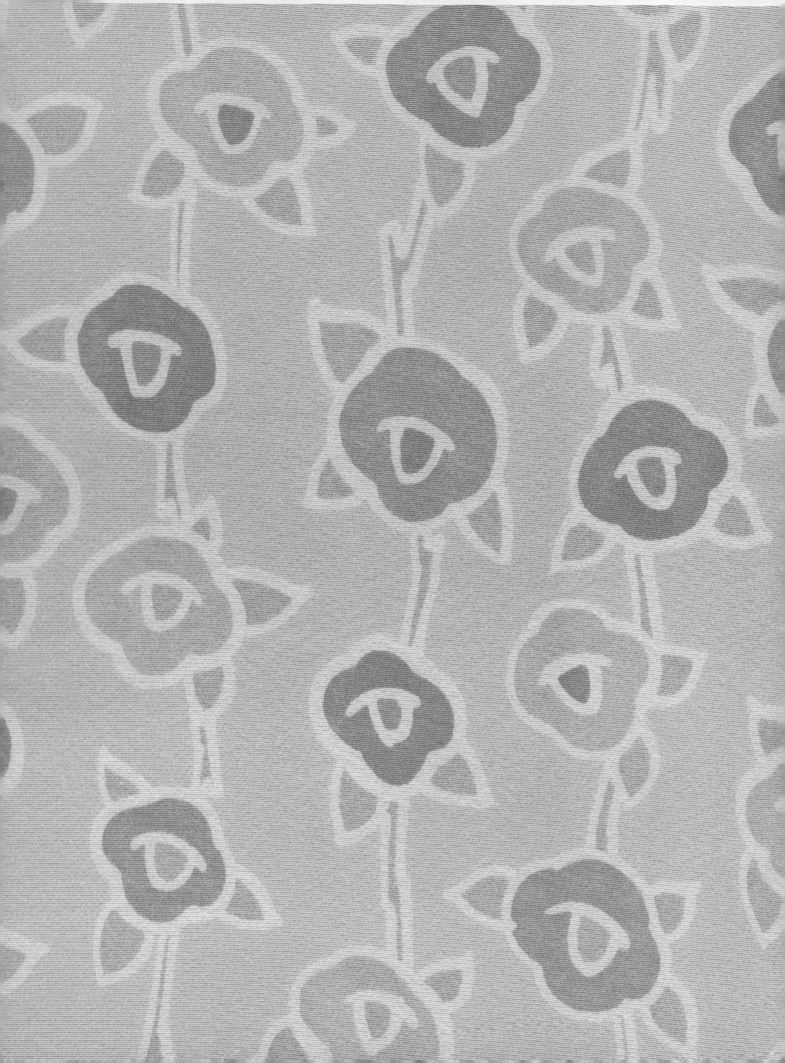

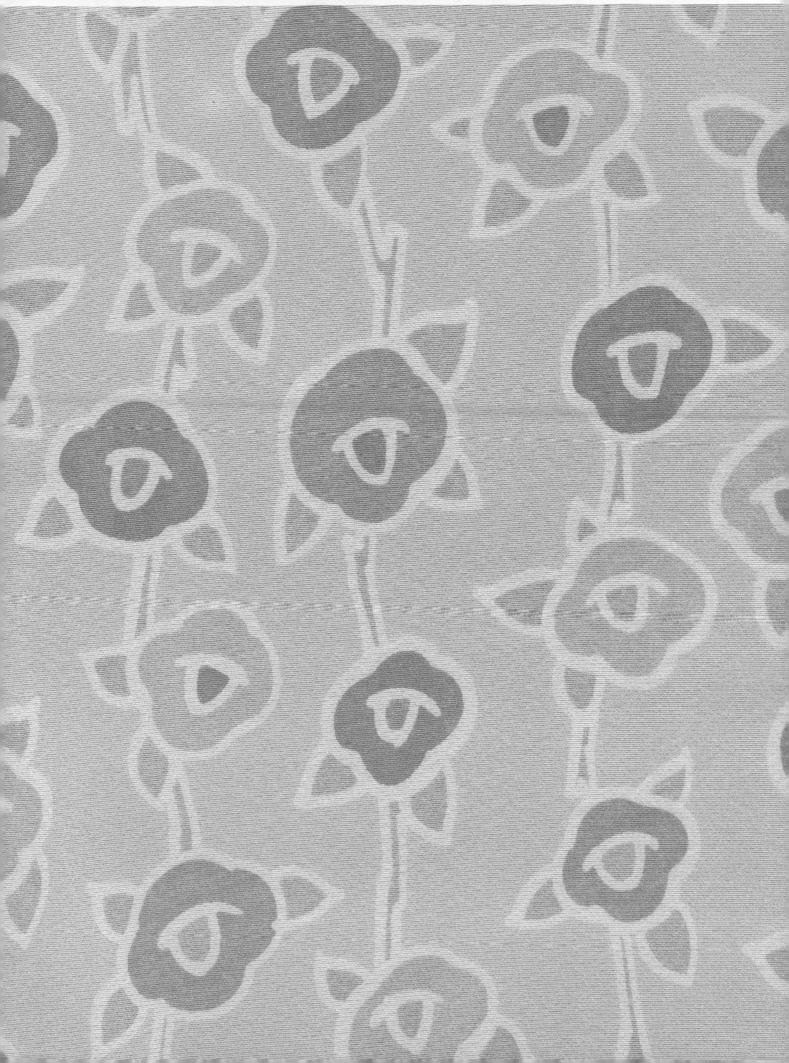